How To Find Your Soulmate

This book provides comprehensive guidance on recognizing genuine love and discerning warning signs within relationships

(Effective Strategies to Implement Today for Securing a Life Partner or Identifying an Ideal Match)

Willie Anderson

TABLE OF CONTENT

A Guide To Recognizing Your Soulmate 1

Life Is A Continuous Cycle Of Cause And Effect. 12

Existence Versus Nonexistence 35

Engage In The Pursuit, And You Shall Encounter Feelings Of Exasperation. 41

Strategies For Manifesting Your Desire To Discover An Ideal Life Partner 61

How To Ascertain If He Harbors An Interest In You 67

Do You Intend Or Desire To Start A Family With Me Following A Single Encounter? 84

Sealing The Deal 127

A Guide To Recognizing Your Soulmate

If one were to observe their surroundings, one would ascertain that there exist various couples who serve as exemplars, substantiating the existence of soulmates. This implies that it is feasible for one to discover and cultivate that desired connection as well, provided they actively seek out relevant indicators. Therefore, how does one determine when they have encountered their soulmate? Take into consideration these eight indicators of a compatible life partner, and you will discern when you have encountered your ideal match.

Discern Your Soulmate's Identity Through these Eight Indicators of Soulmate Connection

You are at ease when expressing your true self.

It is customary to possess a variety of masks that are worn in various situations with the purpose of assimilating or adapting. Nevertheless, one of the most gratifying aspects of being in the company of a soulmate is the absence of necessity for any facade. Instead, one inherently exhibits their true self and it appears as if both individuals are authentically expressing their genuine identities to each other.

Displaying authenticity in this manner allows for deep levels of intimacy, and it is often during the initial encounter that one becomes aware of the remarkable potential present.

You possess a profound intuitive ability.

Frequently, a moment of realization occurs when one encounters their true soulmate. At times, one may experience the phenomenon of instantaneously perceiving love, while on other occasions, it can evoke a profound sense of familiarity.

If you experience a sense of comfort, vitality, and emotional intimacy in the presence of someone despite having recently met them, it is highly probable that this relationship will endure in the long run.

You share the same perspective on the future.

This is a crucial indicator indicating the discovery of one's soulmate since it signifies not only a profound bond but also one of the most dependable predictors of a contented union.

In the event that there is a lack of alignment in essential principles, envisioning a shared vision for the future and pursuing similar aspirations in life, animosity progressively develops and commences to taint the relationship. Therefore, when you encounter an individual who envisions their life unfolding in parallel to your own aspirations, you have undoubtedly stumbled upon a valuable treasure.

You engage in reciprocal challenges

Your ideal partner will not only hold great admiration for your accomplishments, but also broaden your perspective to illuminate the vast potential within you. This can pose a significant challenge as it entails both individuals consistently motivating each other to venture beyond their respective zones of comfort.

However, the unique combination of challenge and support provided by a soulmate is a major catalyst for personal development and growth. Furthermore, in the forthcoming period, it is indeed foreseeable that you will express deep gratitude towards one another for the invaluable support and subtle guidance rendered throughout the course of years!

You are closest companions.

There is a prevalent belief that intimate partners are incapable of cultivating a close friendship.

Nevertheless, in actuality, a robust camaraderie serves as the bedrock for a enduring love affair. Upon encountering your soulmate, you simultaneously encounter your closest confidant and companion.

It remains crucial to cultivate social connections beyond the confines of one's romantic partnership. This signifies that you effortlessly comprehend one another on a profound level, surpassing the typical degree of understanding. Moreover, you share a mutual sense of humor and expeditiously evolve into each other's foremost pillar of support.

You actively strive to maintain and nurture the relationship.

Every partnership entails challenges and disagreements, even in the case of soulmates coming together. Challenges and hurdles will inevitably arise along the way. Regardless of whether one is confronting familial challenges, financial concerns, health issues, professional instability, or parental dilemmas, a pair destined to be united will persistently strive for the preservation of their relationship.

Significantly, you will discover mechanisms for collaborative engagement with the aim of improving the situational dynamics, as both parties will prioritize the preservation of the relationship over the protection of individual egos.

There exists a mutual sense of respect.

Relationships frequently dissolve when individuals attempt to alter one another. In contrast, soulmates exhibit a fundamental level of mutual respect towards one another. Furthermore, this regard is founded upon a genuine understanding of one another, encompassing both strengths and weaknesses.

If you discover that you sincerely embrace an individual despite their idiosyncrasies and psychological tendencies, and you perceive an unwavering acceptance reciprocated towards you, this could potentially signify a profound connection with a soulmate.

One can choose to be separate, but they have a preference for being in each other's company.

Soulmates possess the ability to strike a harmonious equilibrium between periods of togetherness and moments of separation. They place their confidence in one another and maintain a sense of intimacy even while engaging in separate endeavors, rather than succumbing to feelings of envy or apprehension.

Simultaneously, when engaged in a partnership with your soulmate, there is an inherent understanding that one's utmost contentment and sense of purpose are derived from experiencing moments of genuine connection and shared intimacy as a unified pair. If the notion of spending time together ever appears burdensome, it might be beneficial to reflect upon the underlying cause.

In light of everything, what could be more ideal than spending time in the company of one's foremost companion, beloved partner, staunch supporter, and primary collaborator?

Life Is A Continuous Cycle Of Cause And Effect.

The second principle that governs the manifestation of harmonious relationships is the recognition that life serves as a reflection. We have previously touched upon this matter in the earlier sections of the book; however, I feel compelled to delve deeper into it before transitioning to the third and ultimate principle.

Upon my initial relocation to the island of Cyprus, I was taken aback by the lack of courtesy and manners exhibited by the Greek Cypriots. I encountered frequent instances of being abruptly overtaken or experiencing persistent tailgating during my commute to the supermarket, to the extent that it became exceedingly challenging to navigate safely on the highway. Individuals consistently engaged in queue-jumping while the service personnel at various establishments exhibited a perpetual lack of courteous demeanor or inclination to extend smiles. For a significant duration, I staunchly held the perspective that the Cypriots exhibited a pronounced lack of politeness. Subsequently, I established acquaintances with individuals who were native residents of Cyprus. I established a strong rapport with the proprietor of the nearby pharmacy, a highly knowledgeable and amiable individual by the name of Savvas. Soon after our initial encounter, he graciously invited me to partake in a leisurely luncheon, during which we engaged in delightful discourse for a substantial period of three hours. Throughout the majority of the time, he spoke highly of

Cyprus and its inhabitants. He conveyed to me that I am truly fortunate as an individual, as I reside in Cyprus, a land distinguished by its inhabitants' profound capacity for love and compassion. Savvas asserted that it would be an arduous task to encounter individuals who possess a higher degree of compassion and concern than the people of Cyprus, even if I were to embark on a lifelong journey exploring different parts of the globe. Naturally, I did not contest his beliefs; however, it is fair to say that I was not fully aligned with his perspective.

However, an occurrence of an unusual nature subsequently unfolded. During the subsequent weeks, a significant transformation in the behavior and demeanor of the Cypriot individuals became evident to me. They exhibited improved driving skills, shop assistants adopted cheerful dispositions, and unfamiliar individuals on the street extended greetings of goodwill as they crossed paths with me. There exist only two plausible justifications for this shift in paradigm: either a clandestine gathering occurred, wherein the entirety of Cyprus reached a collective consensus to embody enhanced levels of hospitality, or, more probable, the transformation I perceived was not external, but rather an internal evolution within myself.

Life operates as a substantial boomerang, hence it is imperative to exercise caution when releasing anything into the world, for it shall inevitably return to you with great velocity. This principle holds such significance that I designate it as a legal principle. The intended essence of my statement is that regardless of your concurrence, the occurrence in question is inevitable and will transpire irrespective of your standpoint. Analogously, the principle of gravity remains indifferent to the belief or disbelief of individuals.

I possess an acquaintance within my network on the social media platform, Facebook. If I were to compile and provide you with a comprehensive compilation of all her status updates, it is highly probable that you would develop the impression that she endures a rather distressing existence. Upon initial observation, I must concede that she does seem to possess an exceptional streak of misfortune. However, incorporating the principle of the boomerang effect into our perspective renders her circumstances wholly comprehensible and readily predictable. In the event of her need to visit the doctor, her statement would be something akin to "I kindly solicit your well-wishes as I am scheduled for a return appointment with my medical practitioner this afternoon." It is fortuitous that the test results may not be prepared yet, as per my current circumstances. Would you be able to speculate on the content of her forthcoming status update? Allow me to provide you with a hint: kindly remove the acronym "LOL" and substitute it with "FFS," and you will be drawing nearer to grasping the underlying motif of the status.

By harboring the anticipation that the doctor will err during your consultation, you knowingly project a cosmic directive signaling your desire for such outcome. If one were to focus on the difficulties within their marital relationship and perceive their spouse in a negative light, it is possible to observe how this perception gradually solidifies into an increasingly prevalent reality. Seldom do you awaken to find your marriage instantaneously restored. We possess an innate cognitive mechanism endowed with immense creative potential, analogous to a manifestation apparatus. When directed towards a desired goal, this cognitive dynamo brings forth the desired outcome into our reality. When directed towards adversity, it ensnares a multitude of unfortunate occurrences in its gravitational pull, drawing them nearer to one's vicinity. If you direct your efforts towards success or happiness, your life will undergo a transformative and positive shift. Hence, we are all endowed with this mystical armament upon birth, although it arrives devoid of any guidance booklet or protective mechanism. When you direct its attention towards undesirable content, it does not prompt with a query such as "Are you completely certain, esteemed user?" and seek your selection of either "Confirm" or "Cancel."

Herein lies a query for your consideration: what is the outcome when you aim your laser weapon at a void?

You might leap to the conclusion that nothing happens but that is not quite right. Please take note that this particular ray gun has the capability of intensifying and enhancing the subject matter it sets its beam upon. The void within the focal point invariably extends and intensifies. It magnifies a minor void into a substantial abyss, which Nazi concentration camp survivor Victor Frankl denoted as the existential vacuum, or more plainly termed 'human emptiness'. When we engender this emptiness within ourselves, it results in anguish and suffering. We make attempts to alleviate the void with various objects or experiences, aiming to eliminate the sense of emptiness. To what extent do you encounter individuals who exhibit a preoccupation with indulging in opulence within their lifestyles? They want an expensive car to impress the neighbors; they take grand vacations and tell all their friends about how amazing it was, they want a bigger house, designer clothes and all the visible trappings of success that the world can offer. This refers to their persistent efforts to alleviate their inner void through material possessions.

Disposing personal belongings and miscellaneous items into the abyss yields no impact, as the laser firearm remains fixed on a nonexistent target while the gravitational singularity continues to expand ceaselessly. Obtaining material possessions is a pursuit of happiness that is unlikely to yield significant results, much like attempting to fill a volcano by adding a single grain of sand each day. Many individuals seek to bridge the internal void within themselves through the use of substances such as drugs, alcohol, and engagement in sexual activities. They develop an intense preoccupation with either one of these endeavors or often all of them and beyond, under the mistaken conviction that these various aspects and material possessions have the ability to alleviate their suffering. To what extent have you been aware of the instances where prominent individuals in the film and music industry, widely recognized as Hollywood actors and rock stars, seem to possess an abundance of opportunities and fame but tragically meet their demise as a result of deliberate self-inflicted acts, substance abuse, or a combination thereof? However, what could be the explanation for this occurrence in individuals leading seemingly fulfilled lifestyles? It is highly improbable that a universal solution can be universally applied to all circumstances. Each individual enters this world with a distinct purpose, a unique reason for being, and failing to fulfill this purpose will result in a similarly distinctive void.

If you persist in remaining in a job that elicits feelings of intense dissatisfaction, continue to endure a dysfunctional relationship, or hold the belief that your potential for success is limited to its current extent, then you are essentially directing the ray gun towards a void. When individuals heed the call of their innermost conviction and place unwavering faith in their subconscious mind (or one's instinctual intuition, if one so chooses), it illuminates the path towards their profound interests and deepest passions. Rock musicians achieve vast wealth and celebrity status by pursuing their passions and engaging in the pursuit of their true artistic inclinations. Subsequently, they grow fatigued with incessantly producing identical content annually, yet find themselves confined within a particular way of life. The attendees express a strong desire to partake in renowned melodies that they hold dear, and correspondingly, the concert organizers insist that the band cater to the preferences of the paying spectators. Rock musicians transition from pursuing their artistic passion and creating music that resonates with them, to merely becoming revered and idolized performers playing popular songs on demand like an extravagant and admired musical apparatus. They embark on worldwide tours, showcasing their musical prowess in renowned stadiums, adhering to a consistent repertoire performed in an unvarying sequence. Evening after evening, month after month, and year after year. Initially, no expectations were held regarding their abilities, other than pursuing their passion. If we advance beyond the pinnacle of their achievements, it is apparent that they contend with numerous individuals, including an agent, PR representative, concert promoter, former spouse, significant other, and a narcotics supplier. All parties insist on a consistent inflow of funds, akin to what they have previously experienced. They are unable to cease their labor at the sausage factory or even diminish their pace, consequently forfeiting their sense of life's purpose. The emergence and rapid expansion of the cavity reaches such substantial proportions that it cannot be remedied, rendering life devoid of purpose and fraught with anguish.

Each individual is allocated a single ray gun endowed with magical properties. However, it is important to note that this allocation does not come with any accompanying training, instructional documentation, or safety mechanisms. This is the circumstance that requires our attention. You may opt to perceive it as a fortunate occurrence or an unfortunate one; nevertheless, the firearm will simply fulfill its intended purpose. Due to the limited availability of this firearm, its singular focus can only target one entity at any given moment. Consequently, it is implausible to generate additional financial resources whilst simultaneously directing its aim towards the notion that money is scarce and elusive. Unless the focus shifts from being an inadequate performer in this domain, attaining proficiency in public speaking will remain unachievable. If you desire greater confidence, it is advised to maintain a singular focus on attaining such a state and continuously remain cognizant of any inclination towards contemplating the contrary viewpoint.

Evidently, advising you to refrain from contemplating your unsatisfactory marital relationship would yield results comparable to suggesting that you ignore the sensations in your right foot. Prior to my mentioning the "right foot," it is likely that you were completely oblivious to its presence. However, despite my explicit instruction not to fixate on it, you immediately became cognizant of its existence and are quite possibly still conscious of it in this very moment. I acknowledge that it is inevitable for you to continue to experience concern regarding the deteriorating relationship; such apprehension is not only common, but anticipated. Nevertheless, what I implore you to alter is the duration during which you permit the notion to persist. Develop the skill of discerning negative thoughts, recognizing their occurrence, and purposefully envisioning their opposite. Numerous accomplished athletes employ this methodology to refine and augment their performance. Renowned golfer Jack Nicklaus is famously quoted as stating, "I consistently envision a vivid and clear mental image of every shot I take, be it during a practice session or an actual game." Initially, I perceive the ball in the desired position, impeccably pale and elevated on the vivid, emerald green lawn. Subsequently, the scene undergoes a swift transition, whereby my observation shifts to the trajectory, course, and configuration of the ball, even extending to its behavior upon impact. Subsequently, a gradual transition occurs, leading to the subsequent scene wherein I can be seen executing a swing that has the capacity to materialize the preceding images."

In the year of 1992, a study was conducted by Anne Isaac to delve into the impact of mental practice on the advancement of sports skills. Although previous research on this subject matter predominantly demonstrated favorable outcomes of mental rehearsal, it is crucial to note that these studies primarily lacked an examination conducted within a genuine field environment involving participants who acquired tangible athletic abilities rather than mere unfamiliar motor assignments. Isaac resolved this issue in her experiment. Additionally, she conducted experiments to determine whether individuals who possess superior self-representation skills and a heightened level of self-image control exhibit enhanced overall performance levels. Isaac conducted a comprehensive assessment involving a sample size of 78 individuals, subsequently categorizing them into two distinct groups based on their level of expertise in trampolining: novice or experienced trampolinists.

Subsequently, she proceeded to partition the two groups into an experimental and control group. Additionally, she categorized the subjects into high or low imagers, taking into account their initial level of skill. Both cohorts underwent training in three distinct skills throughout a duration of six weeks. To mitigate potential confounds, the experimenter remained unaware of the identity of the imagery group until the conclusion of the study.

The experimental group engaged in a 2-1/2 minute session of physical practice, subsequently followed by a 5-minute period of mental practice. In conclusion, a further 2 and a half minutes of physical rehearsal ensued subsequent to the mental rehearsal. In the interim, the control group engaged in a physical task relating to the skill for a duration of 2 and a half minutes, subsequently followed by a 5-minute session of undertaking a cognitively demanding exercise involving abstract challenges, such as solving mathematical problems, puzzles, and vowel deletion. Subsequently, an additional duration of 2 and a half minutes was allocated for the purpose of engaging in practical exercises related to the skill.

The experiment yielded the following results: there was a noteworthy disparity in the advancement of individuals categorized as high imagers as compared to those categorized as low imagers. In both the novice and experimental cohorts, wherein the initial levels of skill proficiency were comparable, it was found that the high imagery groups exhibited markedly superior enhancements compared to the low imagery group.

The effectiveness of visual imagery can be attributed to the notion that when one envisions themselves executing tasks flawlessly and fulfilling their deepest aspirations, they are effectively establishing tangible neural pathways within their brain, akin to the actual execution of said tasks. These patterns bear resemblance to minuscule imprints in the cerebral cells, capable of facilitating an athlete's physical accomplishments through the sheer act of practicing the maneuver mentally. Therefore, the purpose of mental imagery is to cultivate cognition and establish the neural pathways within our cerebral structure, thereby facilitating the precise execution of desired motor actions.

Prior to engaging in communication with a challenging individual in your professional environment or discussing your emotions with your spouse, it is advisable to contemplate a hypothetical scenario wherein everything transpires flawlessly. Visualize yourself effectively articulating the issues in a composed and content manner—envision, perceive, and experience all the sensations that will manifest when the outcome aligns precisely with your desired expectations. Observe and perceive your partner's response aligning precisely with your desired expectations. Repeatedly perform the task, ensuring that with each iteration, it becomes more vibrant, resonant, vivid, and tangible compared to the preceding one.

You are best advised to place your trust in me on this matter, as my extensive personal experience and the astonishing life transformations observed among the members of my Manifesting Magic club attest to the undeniable efficacy of this very technique.

Existence Versus Nonexistence

To be honest, we are constantly embodying something. The inquiry that should be posed is, "What is my current demeanor or conduct?" If one lacks awareness of this, it is imperative to direct one's focus accordingly. Exhibiting enthusiasm and fervor is preferable to displaying anger and despondency. The emotional state in which you find yourself will ultimately determine the things you draw towards you. You consistently draw individuals, situations, and environments in accordance with your prevailing state of existence. The query once more arises: "In what manner am I presently comporting myself?" Truly, this is where the true potential lies - within one's immediate sphere of existence, whether it be a conscious decision to manifest a particular state of being, or an unwitting adherence to a passive existence, allowing external circumstances to dictate one's experience of life.

Despite the primary focus of this literary work on the pursuit of an ideal romantic partner, its ultimate purpose lies in the introspective journey of reshaping one's self-connection. That marks the inception of the pursuit for one's soulmate.

Individuals present in our lives serve as reflections of ourselves. They consistently mirror our emotions and state of being. If we constantly attract outcomes based on our thoughts, emotions, and feelings, it is in our best interest to consciously select our state of being. The state of happiness exudes a significant allure to individuals of the opposite gender, not solely in terms of energy.

During my twenties, a period characterized by prolonged solitude, I pondered the probability of discovering a suitable partner, or alternatively, resigning myself to a solitary existence. This genuine apprehension was not only limited to me but may likely be shared by numerous individuals. When assuming a certain role or state, such as when immersed in fear, it becomes evident that fear is undeniably one of the emotional states we are capable of encountering. In contemporary times, it appears that fear is being actively propagated through various media outlets. Succumbing to this pervasive fear can result in the Law of Attraction working in such a way that we attract further circumstances and conditions that generate feelings of fear.

In contrast, embracing an attitude of affection will inevitably draw forth conditions and circumstances that facilitate the further cultivation and encounter of love. Undoubtedly, love possesses unparalleled potency. It may appear straightforward or commonplace, yet it is often the case that we fail to recognize the inherent potency of prioritizing love as the initial approach.

In general, our endeavors in life are usually pursued through active engagement. Action may be effective, however, it is often our tendency to exert excessive effort by taking further action, in order to achieve desired outcomes, even without acknowledging or resolving our emotional state or energetic disposition. When we experience love, excitement, passion, or any elevated emotional state, we effectively enhance our ability to draw towards us that which we truly desire to attract. As previously mentioned, I had not been actively seeking companionship during that period. Nevertheless, I was emanating a certain energy that eventually drew situations, occurrences, and individuals towards me, all of which resonated with that particular energy.

Therefore, by demonstrating attentiveness to your own existence, you can enhance your prospects of discovering a kindred spirit, while simultaneously fostering the ability to allure other aspirations that may be dear to you.

Engage In The Pursuit, And You Shall Encounter Feelings Of Exasperation.

During the aforementioned program, wherein the talk show host unveiled the crafty tactics employed by certain individuals in their initial encounters with women, he invited a woman in her early forties who harbored a deep longing to comprehend the reasons behind her lack of success in forming a romantic partnership.

As it transpired, she had experienced a sense of desperation since her early twenties. The host also featured three of her former partners from the past two decades (despite having numerous others), and each of them attested that she commenced exerting pressure for a marital commitment at an early stage in their relationship.

In addition to her failure to adhere to the principles outlined in this book, a significant error on her part was the deliberate pursuit of her perfect life partner.

The scripture states, 'Those who actively seek shall surely uncover.'

In a manner similar to devout individuals who often interpret Bible passages in a misguided fashion, someone uttering this retort is clearly misapprehending its intended meaning. In our culture, a considerable number of women pursue the goal of obtaining a suitable partner by engaging with multiple individuals, often ranging from several to numerous, and evaluating their potential for committing to a committed and enduring relationship.

If one wishes to perpetuate the experience of a recurrently wounded heart, they may proceed to conform to prevailing societal norms. If that is not the case, then you must cease displaying such a sense of desperation.

The illusion of control

Indeed, the crux of the matter lies in exercising control. Women who actively pursue the search for their soul mate believe that they possess agency in the process of finding their ideal partner. You possess no additional influence or authority over that matter as much as you lack control over the occurrence of rainfall today.

To put it differently, you lack any form of authority or influence. This fact instills fear in numerous unmarried women. However, it must be acknowledged that regardless of one's spiritual convictions, there exists a formidable force within the universe that surpasses individual capabilities.

Indeed, it is imperative to undertake necessary measures to attain one's objectives or life aspirations. However, these endeavors should be rooted in trust and not driven by apprehension. The level of control exerted over one's life is indicative of the dominance of fear over faith within an individual. The greater the exertion of control in matters of romantic involvement, the higher the likelihood of experiencing heartbreak.

One can pursue a romantic partner without compromising their emotional welfare. How can one effectively strike a balance and maintain a sense of control without succumbing to obsessively micromanaging the situation? If you are prepared to receive unconventional guidance, which challenges the conventional wisdom offered by the majority of existing relationship literature, please continue reading.

The nightlife environment is having a detrimental impact on your well-being.

A widely favored destination among individuals seeking romantic encounters is the nocturnal establishment commonly known as a night club, encompassing within its purview the omnipresent bar, or for the benefit of my British audience, a pub. There are two significant challenges associated with this, disregarding any ethical concerns that individuals of faith may hold (although these concerns are indeed significant, my intent here is not to impart sermons).

Initially, it is evident that a significant number, possibly constituting the majority, of the individuals who frequent certain establishments are in search of casual encounters. Due to the fact that the average man who loiters in nightclubs often possesses manipulative tendencies and preys upon vulnerable women who are easily exploited, it would be highly advisable for you, as my girlfriend, to steadfastly refrain from frequenting such establishments.

The second factor that prohibits individuals from meeting their soul mates within the night club scene is the likelihood of actively seeking such a connection if one chooses to partake in this environment. What is the likelihood of encountering your ideal partner within the premises of a nightlife establishment? Faithful, responsible, willing to commit, sober…hmmm. I don't think so. All possibilities are conceivable, however, we are addressing the matter of your life. Are you genuinely prepared to assume such a substantial level of risk?

If your attempts to find a compatible partner through clubs have yielded nothing but disappointment and heartache, it is high time to alter your approach.

Online for divorce

Undoubtedly, amidst the demands and pace of contemporary life, numerous individuals who are not in committed relationships lack the necessary time or vitality to engage in socializing at nightclubs following their professional obligations. They opt to engage in online dating platforms.

It has come to my knowledge that a select number of contentedly married couples have indeed established their acquaintances through online platforms and subsequently arranged an initial meeting facilitated by an online dating service. However, a considerable number of couples who enter marriage after making initial contact through online platforms ultimately find themselves seeking dissolution through legal proceedings. Why? Due to the prevalence of virtual communication, individuals can maintain a facade, concealing their true selves for extended periods of time. It is not uncommon for men to resort to unethical tactics, going to great lengths to emotionally manipulate women into developing feelings for them.

I was acquainted with a married pair who epitomized the inherent risks associated with engaging in online dating. She possessed a slender figure, exhibited considerable allure, and hailed from a foreign nation. He had a significant excess weight, a diagnosis of diabetes, and was experiencing mental health challenges. She developed feelings for him prior to having any visual knowledge of his appearance, and was unaware of his mental health condition until after they had exchanged marital vows.

They subsequently dissolved their marriage after several years. Upon discovering this fact, I experienced a substantial sense of alleviation on behalf of the woman, whose age I noted to be only a few years junior to mine. The extent of suffering and stress she had to endure throughout the duration of the marriage is beyond my capacity to fathom.

However, I can strongly recommend that we engage in photograph exchange." "However, I possess exceptional skill in interpreting underlying messages.

Whatever. With the exception that a reputable online dating platform will actively filter out individuals demonstrating questionable traits, utilizing such a service bears resemblance to frequenting establishments such as night clubs, as it exposes oneself to elevated vulnerability and potential emotional distress due to the desire to exert control over the type of individuals encountered.

Lend me your ears, my dear companion, it is commendable to possess a general notion of the qualities one deems necessary in a gentleman, as well as those that one refuses to tolerate. As an illustration, it is more likely that your overall happiness will be enhanced by entering into a relationship with a man who demonstrates sound fiscal management and abstains from drug use, compared to the alternative scenario. However, should your sole priority lie in encountering a gentleman who shares your preferences in terms of culinary choices, literary material, auditory preferences, and athletic pursuits, it is plausible that you might overlook the opportunity to find your ideal companion and destined counterpart.

Even if one does not exhibit excessive selectivity, solely relying on online dating as the primary means of finding a partner may lead to overlooking one's ideal match. Upon our initial encounter, during which our inaugural rendezvous transpired shortly before the Yuletide season, it became apparent that Jerry had already conveyed to his kin that he had grown wearisome of his solitary existence and was desirous of establishing a profound companionship. Several months after our affection blossomed, Jerry's brother brought to my attention that he had intended to bestow upon Jerry a subscription to a religiously-oriented internet matchmaking platform for the approaching Christmas! Conversely, I had firmly resolved never to avail myself of such a service.

What could have been our current situation if Jerry had chosen to remain at home, engaging in online browsing of profiles in search of potential romantic partners? I am of the belief that it is possible that God, in due course, would have orchestrated our union; nonetheless, He permits us to endure the repercussions stemming from our actions driven by fear. It is possible that we are both single - or perhaps involved in unsuitable marriages.

What if you were to utilize a professional matchmaking service such as "It's Just Lunch" or exclusively opt for a service that assists in connecting you with individuals with whom you share common interests? To state it differently, you abstain from participating in an online social connection that has the potential to mislead or disappoint you, and instead solely employ the Internet as a means to interact with individuals in person? This presents a clearly more secure situation as compared to the one that the woman, who unknowingly wedded an individual with mental illness, unfortunately encountered. However, the core essence remains centered around your concerted efforts to establish authority.

Moreover, even in the event that an individual registered on an online dating platform has undergone background checks, they still have the capacity to present a deceptive facade when encountered in person. I am indifferent to the extent of religiosity associated with the service. May I disclose the truth to you? I have encountered numerous individuals who identify themselves as followers of the Christian faith whom I would strongly discourage anyone from pursuing a romantic relationship with, let alone considering marriage.

In my envisioned utopia, I would prefer to witness the cessation of all dating activities.

Please take a moment to compose yourself and prepare to hear me elaborate on this unconventional statement.

Dating is deadly

Prior to proceeding further, it is essential that we establish a mutual understanding of the term 'date' within the contextual framework of searching for a lifelong companion. As it may be presumed that my intent is to discourage any individual from engaging in one-on-one outings with a male counterpart, I feel compelled to clarify my viewpoint. This is not so.

Let us commence by referring to the definition provided in my spouse's antiquated unabridged Webster's

Dictionary: "a prearranged social commitment, encounter, or occasion with an individual of the opposite sex." It is evident that this source is outdated. Nowadays, however, it is commonplace to schedule a rendezvous with one's girlfriend for a midday meal, or with a professional associate or patron for an evening repast, or even with a romantic prospect who shares the same gender.

You may be curious as to the issue with the term "date", as defined above. Nothing besides the prevalent usage in contemporary society, particularly in the pursuit of finding a compatible life partner, wherein dating is understood as engaging in social interactions with individuals of the opposite gender. Given the significance of this definition in present times, it is the one I will adopt for our intended objectives.

When engaging in the activity of dating, it suggests that you are partaking in exclusive one-on-one encounters with multiple gentlemen, either sequentially or concurrently. According to certain literary sources, this is purportedly an ordinary facet of existence and intended to be enjoyable. It is your prerogative to pursue romantic relationships with multiple individuals until you enter into a committed engagement. It would be prudent to refrain from exclusively aligning yourself with a single individual until you have received a clear and unequivocal declaration of their commitment. In addition, how will you ascertain your predispositions without engaging in romantic encounters with multiple individuals?

The aforementioned points, namely the notion that dating serves as a means of diversion and as a tool for understanding one's compatibility with diverse individuals, can be perceived as the benefits of engaging in romantic relationships. Furthermore, you will receive an added benefit of a complimentary meal, movie, or beverage as an additional incentive. However, those are the only benefits.

I once heard someone on the radio express the notion that dating serves as a preparatory ground for potential marital separation. Consider this: you consent to accompany an individual on an outing. You both share feelings of mutual attraction, consequently reaching a consensus to engage in another social encounter. And again. And again. Primarily, you engage in solitary experiences during your outings, and exclusively encounter one another within the confines of contrived – albeit pleasurable – situations. If you do not adhere to a religious doctrine that condemns premarital sexual activity, it is probable that you engage in sexual relations with every man you date beyond the initial few encounters.

You start to feel emotionally attached to him, until one day he shows a side of himself you don't like, or vice versa, and one or the other of you decides that you want to stop dating. And your heart shatters – or, at the very least, encounters disillusionment and vexation.

Once you have overcome this situation, you proceed to engage with another individual who possesses qualities such as attractiveness or wealth, and go through a similar sequence again. One should recognize that in the context of romantic relationships, it is frequently observed that both individuals engage in strategic behaviors, attempting to influence and mold the other person according to their desired perception of an ideal companion.

You believe that you can exert influence over the process of finding your soul mate by consciously selecting prospective partners from contextually favorable settings, such as social gatherings or nightlife venues. However, instead of encountering your destined Soulmate, you are confronted with distress and sadness.

Your propensity to exert excessive control over this process is detrimentally impacting your well-being, incrementally and gradually. And you will experience an even greater emotional distress if you resemble the distressed woman I witnessed on the televised talk show, who exerted undue pressure on her romantic prospects to establish a commitment at an early stage of their relationship.

What measures do you employ to circumvent this suffering? How does one encounter their ideal life partner, if not by means of engaging in dating?

Please secure your seatbelt, as the information I am about to disclose has the potential to astonish you. It will be contrary to the prevailing currents of mainstream culture, please bear this in mind.

Strategies For Manifesting Your Desire To Discover An Ideal Life Partner

Dreams frequently depict concealed truths, aspirations, anxieties, and yearnings residing within the depths of the human subconscious. Adolescents and individuals with an inclination towards romance often harbor fantasies about the person they consider to be their ideal life partner and soul mate, eagerly yearning for their manifestation in the realm of reality.

During intimate conversations with acquaintances or coworkers, it is common to hear a shared desire emerge time and again: the longing for an ideal companion in matters of romance. "However, a significant portion of individuals lack the knowledge or direction required to initiate the process.

and what to anticipate in their ideal romantic partner. It is imperative that you possess a clearly defined mental image. For instance, you should be able to describe the primary qualities that you are looking for in your life partner.

Certain individuals desire intellectually astute and adept companions, who possess the capacity to alleviate our economic obligations and provide unwavering assistance during familial adversities. Certain individuals desire individuals who are lively and amiable, capable of eliciting laughter from others. There are those who desire affluent companions, individuals who possess the means to purchase lavish gifts and accompany us on extravagant vacations. Certain individuals who are deeply infatuated may desire passionate romantics who will lavish us with bouquets of roses, accompany us to intimate candlelit dinners, and repeatedly utter those three enchanting words. It is essential to establish your objectives prior to embarking on an unwavering pursuit for a romantic partner.

Relationships are not solely established through romantic and sexual inclinations; they also necessitate cultivating friendship, compatibility, and mutual comprehension. Given that a relationship is based solely on the strong physical chemistry between partners, it is possible that one may become weary of it over time, resulting in diverging perspectives and consistent disagreements. It is advisable to establish your relationship on a foundation of trust and camaraderie, rather than relying solely on physical attractiveness.

A relationship entails an enduring bond forged by the shared experiences, intertwining lives, and harmonized lifestyles over a significant span of time. You embark on a shared journey, traversing the peaks and valleys of life in unison – united as one, providing mutual support and embracing a level of commitment that should be shared with your life partner.

Identifying the appropriate individual is merely the initial step. It is imperative to gradually establish a connection by fostering trust, demonstrating care, cultivating love, showing respect, expressing affection, making sacrifices, fostering hope, and upholding faith in order to build a successful relationship. Even the most ideal couple may dissolve if they do not exert effort to sustain and enliven their relationship. Regrettably, a considerable number of individuals acquire life's lessons through arduous paths, subsequent to the loss of beloved ones as a result of their own inadvertence. While certain individuals engage in a cycle of transitioning from one relationship to another, consistently discovering shortcomings within each companion and yearning to reunite with a former partner despite being involved with someone new.

It is imperative to acknowledge that genuine happiness emanates from within oneself, rather than being contingent upon the presence of a partner. If one possesses virtuous qualities, they tend to naturally attract individuals of similar virtue, and conversely, those who lack such qualities. Contemplating the existence of a life partner is permissible, for it is within the realm of the cognitive faculties encompassed by the laws governing creation. Your dreams encompass the fabric of profound ideas that, when intertwined with your vibrant imagination and unwavering ardor, generate a formidable cosmic force capable of transforming those dreams into a transcendent actuality.

If your fantasies happen to be true, may the entire cosmos conspire to aid you in discovering the ideal life partner in this existence.

How To Ascertain If He Harbors An Interest In You

In a genuine romantic bond, the beloved individual is afforded the liberty to express their true self – embracing moments of laughter shared with me, while never resorting to mockery; shedding tears alongside me, yet never on account of me; cherishing life, their own self, and the experience of receiving affection. A relationship founded on the premise of freedom is inherently incompatible with a heart consumed by jealousy and is therefore incapable of thriving. Buscaglia

There are few occurrences that elicit both pleasure and concern to the same extent as developing romantic feelings for someone and being uncertain of their reciprocal affection. Indeed, there is an inherent thrill in developing intense affections for another individual, where even the most ordinary aspects of one's daily life become imbued with fascination and exhilaration due to the overwhelming wave of elation that has now enveloped one's existence. However, one is constantly burdened by the pervasive unease of being deeply infatuated with another individual while simultaneously questioning their own reciprocation of affection.

We get it. When one is fully immersed in the overwhelming fervor of anxious anticipation, each incidental touch, impromptu message, or digital affirmation on a social media platform may appear to hold significance, potentially serving as a determining factor in discerning the possibility of a mutually predetermined future. Certainly, this could potentially result in extended periods of anxious and meticulous examination and reflection, possibly spanning hours, days, weeks, or even months. While a certain level of excessive scrutiny can provide amusement, such as when you and your acquaintances engage in lively intellectual discussions during brunch, resembling a group of passionate scholars, it can also become rather burdensome.

Fortunately, there exist various strategies to ascertain the status of your relationship without resorting to sharing every single text message with your friends for their analysis and expertise. While one may potentially seek outdated dating counsel from parental figures or attempt to decipher astrological compatibility, the optimal course of action lies in attaining guidance from accredited experts.

While Ashley Starwood, a clinical social therapist, asserts that the optimal course of action is to be forthright and express one's emotions in order to avoid miscommunication and obtain clarification, it must be acknowledged that the direct approach may not suit everyone. If you would rather embark on the path of ~carefully interpreting the signs~ prior to baring your soul, you have arrived at the ideal location. Below, we present a selection of definitive indicators that could aid in discerning his sentiments towards you.

1. He is touching you.

Typically, males tend to exhibit a slightly greater inclination towards physicality compared to females. Therefore, when a gentleman endeavors to make physical contact with you in situations where such interaction is unnecessary, it often serves as a useful indicator of his affection towards you. When he desires to underscore something, and he intentionally makes physical contact with your hand or inadvertently brushes against you with his knee, these gestures typically serve as subtle indicators of his genuine emotions.

2. He retains minute particulars concerning your persona.

If you have encountered him on several occasions and he has meticulously retained specific aspects of your prior discussions, it carries significance. When he possesses a fondness for you, he will exhibit heightened attentiveness towards your words as he endeavors to unravel an underlying significance and foster a profound bond.

3. You both have established a connection on social media platforms.

It is not advisable for gentlemen to send friendship requests to ladies with whom they do not share a pre-existing relationship as friends or family, or for whom they do not harbor feelings of mutual affinity. Additional indicators on social media that demonstrate his intention to advance the relationship include showing appreciation for your photographs by 'liking' them or initiating private messaging conversations with you.

4. He maintains direct eye contact with you.

stock

Your recently developed romantic interest may be deliberately seeking direct eye contact with you as a nonverbal means of expressing affection towards you. Should he consistently sustain eye contact with you, it indicates a level of interest on his part. However, should he divert his gaze from you and instead engage in scanning the surroundings, it is possible that his attention is not fixated upon you, signaling a lack of interest, thus allowing you to resume communication with other individuals via text.

5. He demonstrates a level of active engagement during your discussions.

If an individual harbors feelings for you, they will exert effort to engage in conversation with you. What initially appears as an unpleasant conversation has the potential to evolve into a valuable occasion for forging a deeper acquaintance. Occasionally, men may find themselves unsure of how to contribute to the discussion. However, they ultimately demonstrate their engagement through active listening skills and the manner in which they express themselves. If there is a perceptible decline in his vocal tone during your conversation, it is improbable that he possesses an interest in you. However, if his vocal tone is resonant and commanding, and he is actively inquiring about your thoughts and opinions, it is highly probable that he harbors romantic feelings for you as well.

6. He is exhibiting body language associated with dominant or leadership behavior.

Your new acquaintance intends to demonstrate his capability to assume leadership and provide care for you. If he maintains an upright posture, retracts his abdomen, aligns his shoulders, and exudes self-assurance while moving, it serves as a commendable indication of his affections towards you.

7. He inquires about your current relationship status.

iStock

It is quite apparent that if he inquires about your relationship status by asking,

"Are you currently seeing someone?" then it can be inferred that he is indeed interested in pursuing a romantic relationship with you. Nevertheless, few gentlemen are inclined to exhibit such candor. Conversely, they will pose indirect inquiries to ascertain the information. Perhaps he will indicate his single status with the hope of eliciting a reciprocal acknowledgment of singleness on your part.

8. He experiences envy when you engage in conversation with other males.

When engaged in conversations with other males, be it through online communication or face-to-face interactions, your crush may redirect their attention towards you, exhibiting curiosity regarding the nature of your exchanges. A gentleman with no genuine interest in your company would not invest his attention in observing your interactions with other gentlemen during conversations. Don't worry, as soon as you indicate that you just have eyes for him with a great, gorgeous grin, he's sure to be all yours again.

9. He is eager to provide you with support and aid in resolving your difficulties.

Men possess inherent problem-solving abilities. Furthermore, in regards to the individual they are developing romantic feelings for, they strive to identify resolutions for any challenges that may arise. If one articulates a matter of concern, and he harbors affection for you, it is probable that he will diligently search his intellect in pursuit of solutions. A gentleman who possesses affection for you will willingly go the extra distance. They will strive to embody the role of the valiant hero who saves the day.

10. He seeks your reciprocal reaction when he pokes fun or shares a humorous remark.

This recommendation is particularly useful to consider when you find yourself in the company of a close-knit social circle. If he proffers a statement to the collective or endeavors to share a jest, followed by a surreptitious gaze in your direction to observe your reaction, it serves as a remarkable indication of his attraction towards you! This implies that he is yearning for your validation or striving to make a favorable impression upon you.

11. He is conveying his forthcoming plans to you.

If he is expressing aspirations for the future that extend beyond mere professional advancement, it is plausible that his affection for you is genuine. What might be the reasons behind this? As he may potentially envision you being a part of his future, he is seeking to ascertain if you align with his aspirations and objectives.

12. He drunk calls you.

There is a common adage that goes: "In vino veritas," which translates to "In wine, there is truth." This sentiment holds true in the given situation, as alcohol often has the ability to compel individuals to express their genuine emotions. In the event that they make phone calls or send messages to you while under the influence, it can be inferred that they hold a favorable opinion of you (although one should exercise caution towards late-night attempts solely driven by physical desire).

13. He alters his demeanor in your presence.

Males exhibit distinct responses to stress compared to females. However, if their behavior deviates from the usual pattern, such as engaging in increased or decreased conversation, it is probable that the individual harbors feelings for you but lacks the ability to effectively communicate them.

14. He dressed to impress.

It's simple. No woman desires to accompany a man of disheveled appearance for an outing. If he invests additional attention to his grooming or dons high-quality cologne in your presence, it can be reasonably inferred that a man harbors affection for you.

15. He extends an invitation to purchase items for you.

An excellent approach to determine a man's affection for you is by observing his willingness to treat you to a meal or extend support during times of financial hardship. He desires to attend to the welfare of his cherished partner and ensure her continued happiness.

16. His companions depart, leaving the two of you in solitude.

If, in the event that you visit his place of residence and his acquaintances depart, it is highly likely that he harbors feelings of affection towards you. Why? As he has disclosed his sentiments towards you to his acquaintances, he is now seeking an opportunity to spend quality time in solitude.

17. He provides backing to you in the face of unfavorable criticism.

Similar to women, men tend to exhibit possessive tendencies when it concerns their partners. If a man behaves up at a bar or his pals won't give up tormenting you, don't be shocked if your crush jumps to your rescue. It is not only greatly pleasing, but also serves as exemplary proof of his genuine feelings.

18. He is your most exceptional companion when you are indisposed or experiencing discomfort.

From a biological standpoint, males inherently possess the inclination to provide assistance to those in their immediate vicinity. If your newly acquainted significant other extends an offer to retrieve soup, ginger ale, or other delightful indulgences for you in times of minor ailments such as a mild cold, it is an unequivocal indicator that an affectionate bond has been established.

Do You Intend Or Desire To Start A Family With Me Following A Single Encounter?

You have recently completed your college education, relocated to a bustling urban center, and secured gainful employment in your chosen profession. A refined, aesthetically pleasing gentleman extends an invitation to you, which you graciously embrace. During the encounter, you inquire about his background, and he avoids superficial conversation and proceeds directly to the substantive matter. At the age of 35, he has grown weary of his solitary status. His aspirations involve matrimony and starting a family of two children before reaching the age of 37.

It does not require exceptional mathematical prowess to deduce that his primary intention is to expedite the marriage process in order to align with his desired timeline effectively. As an individual who has recently graduated college at the age of 22, I find the notion of entering into matrimony at this juncture to be preposterous. You currently lack the necessary preparedness for engaging in such a significant level of commitment. You desire to embark on a few years of experiences and explorations prior to establishing a domestic life and starting a family.

Looking ahead by a decade, it is apparent that you remain unattached and are currently experiencing a sense of urgency in seeking a life partner who shares the aspiration of marriage and the desire to have two children within a short timeframe. Despite disregarding the 35-year-old individual years ago due to their directness during your past date, you now discover yourself exhibiting the same directness when going on first dates. You consistently observe that these individuals are in a dissimilar phase of life, lacking preparedness for genuine dedication.

Initially, you were unprepared, and presently, you are unable to encounter any prospective suitors with intentions of settling down. What's going on here?

Renowned psychologist Daniel Levinson formulated the "Seasons of Life" theory, which delineates distinct life stages that adults traverse.

Early Adult Transition (Ages 17–22): You undergo the transition into adulthood and make the decision to either pursue higher education by enrolling in a college or university, or embark on a professional career by entering the workforce. You are now permitted to depart from your household and commence your inaugural committed romantic association.

Transitioning into Adulthood (Ages 22–28): Individuals begin to appraise their identity, chart their aspirations, and evaluate their core principles in life.

Maturing into the Thirties (Ages 28–33): As one enters this age bracket, significant shifts in lifestyle may occur, such as embarking on marriage or embracing parenthood.

Establishing Stability (Ages 33-40): During this period, individuals undertake the process of setting a structured lifestyle, attaining objectives, and exhibiting characteristics typically associated with a refined level of adulthood. You may already have assumed the role of a parent and therefore shoulder a greater array of responsibilities in your life.

Mid-life Transition period, occurring between the ages of 40 and 45, entails a comprehensive introspection and potential reevaluation of life choices, encompassing values and the envisioned future. During this period, it is possible for individuals to undergo a divorce or to pursue a career change.

Transitioning into the phase of Middle Adulthood (Ages 45-50), individuals experience a pivotal moment wherein they begin to deliberate upon their forthcoming path and contemplate the enduring impact they will have on future generations.

Pinnacle of Middle Adulthood (Ages 50–60): You may attain the conclusion of your professional career and craft strategies for entering the retirement phase.

Late Adulthood (Age 60): During this stage, individuals engage in introspection, contemplating upon the various choices they have made throughout their lives.

At the age of 22, individuals may not possess the inclination to establish a long-term commitment, however, their readiness for such a commitment may potentially unfold with the passage of time, perhaps around the age of 30. It is highly essential to engage in relationships with individuals who are in a comparable phase of life to ensure effective time management for both parties. The exact age boundaries may vary for each stage, however, it is imperative to ascertain that the individual you are in a relationship with aligns with your current stage.

My youthful appearance deceives them all My cherubic countenance deceives them all My innocently angelic visage deceives them all

I have consistently appeared youthful, which tends to attract the attention of younger individuals. Even family members whom I have been acquainted with throughout my entire existence are astounded upon discerning my actual age. Upon my completion of college, acquaintances of my parents had mistakenly presumed that I had achieved the completion of junior high education. I am consistently being asked to provide identification at all venues, including when attending movie screenings that require viewers to be of a certain age as specified by the film's rating. It is quite fascinating to witness the extent to which individuals can misconstrue my true age.

It proves challenging within the realm of dating to be regarded as a youthful woman rather than a mature individual. I frequently encounter romantic advances from adolescents, necessitating my courteous reminders regarding the inappropriateness of their actions. I have been approached romantically by individuals who do not meet the minimum legal age requirement for operating a motor vehicle. I commend them for their audacious approach to dating; however, I consistently decline.

During my early adulthood, it was not uncommon for others to mistake me for someone who had just reached legal age, as I possessed a youthful appearance that belied my actual age. Indeed, I portrayed a secondary school student in numerous television series. They greatly appreciated having me as a supporting cast member due to my legal age, yet youthful appearance that defied a ten-year age difference. In the midst of engaging in professional endeavors within that particular setting, I received invitations for social outings from a diverse range of gentlemen. If the individuals were present without the accompaniment of a guardian, it can be inferred that they must have been at least 18 years of age.

I decided to afford these individuals an opportunity. Why not? They were in the prime of their sexual maturity, while I lacked experience and eagerly embraced novel experiences. My initial course of action was to request the presentation of their license. Under no circumstances was I going to engage in a romantic relationship with an individual who was under the legal age. Once we ascertained their age to be 18, we proceeded to arrange and initiate a romantic relationship.

Here's to you, Mrs. Robinson

One individual among these eighteen-year-olds, referred to as Charlie, was still pursuing their secondary education. His parents permitted our relationship without being aware that I am 25 years of age. As one grows older, a seven-year gap between individuals becomes negligible. Nevertheless, the realms of a high school student and a young professional are distinct.

Undeniably attractive, he lacked any familiarity with women due to his upbringing in a rigid Catholic household. Our interaction merely consisted of a kiss, during which he openly acknowledged that I was his inaugural encounter in matters of affection. He boasted to his acquaintances about being in a romantic relationship with an older woman, and the news quickly reached his parents. Fortunately, I was never acquainted with them. It is highly likely that they would have taken hostile action towards me had they been aware of my age. Charlie and I had to conclude our romantic relationship, albeit the time we spent together was enjoyable.

Transporting oneself back to the college years

I, too, had a romantic involvement with Sam during my twenty-fifth year. He was 18 and just starting college. He experienced a sense of elevated admiration among his peers on campus due to his relationship with a woman of an older age. He escorted me to fraternity gatherings, and I experienced a deep sense of social disconnection. Undoubtedly, it remained unknown to others that I was out of place, yet it was an awareness that I possessed. Being in his presence evoked a sense of nostalgia, transporting me back to the days of my university years. Attending college was an exhilarating experience, however, I no longer felt accustomed to that particular milieu. Sam and I were in a brief romantic relationship; however, it quickly deteriorated. I found it untenable to continue pursuing relationships with individuals of high school or college age.

Transport me to a future dimension

Shortly following my encounter with Sam, I had the pleasure of crossing paths with a gentleman of great refinement by the name of David. On this occasion, I had the company of an individual who was seven years my senior. I perceived this as precisely the solution I sought!

David, an astute and accomplished businessperson, lavished me with regal treatment. He graciously entertained me, treating me to exquisite meals and showcasing the finest attractions of the locality. I was relieved of the responsibility of monitoring his curfew or attending to his intoxicated college acquaintances. He exhibited a level of maturity and sophistication that was refreshing, making him a welcome departure from my prior romantic involvements.

I attended a Memorial Day gathering accompanied by David, and subsequently observed him engaging in conversation with his male acquaintances. Upon thoroughly surveying the backyard, I immediately experienced a sense of displacement yet again. Instead of dealing with intoxicated college students, there was an abundance of young children scurrying about, creating utter pandemonium. Given that David was in his thirties, it was apparent that all of his acquaintances had entered into matrimony and had children. I endeavored to establish a friendly connection with the women, but they were engrossed in profound discussions pertaining to pregnancy and child-rearing. I had no further contributions to make.

David would have been an excellent match for a woman who prioritizes child-rearing as her primary objective in life. He displayed traits of benevolence and generosity, however, our compatibility was lacking. I was not yet prepared to enter into a committed lifestyle during that period, whereas he expressed a strong desire to initiate a family without delay. We engaged in an extensive discussion regarding our individual life aspirations, ultimately arriving at a mutual agreement to terminate our relationship.

Conclusively, engaging in a romantic relationship with an individual during their high school or college years when you have surpassed that stage proves to be an unproductive use of one's time.

You and the other individuals are at varying life stages, and it would be beneficial for you to seek companionship among those who are more aligned with your age group. The aforementioned statement also holds true when it comes to engaging in a romantic relationship with an individual significantly advanced in age. In the event that you still wish to partake in endeavors, while the other party is prepared for matrimony, it is imperative to initiate early discourse concerning this matter.

Is she engaging in an amorous activity with her grandfather?

I attended a social gathering and occupied a seat on the sofa alongside several individuals. I initiated a conversation with the lady seated adjacent to me. Her name was Jessica. She possessed remarkable beauty and undeniable charm while recounting the extravagant celebration held in honor of her 25th birthday. A significantly elder gentleman was seated beside her, and intermittently, he would softly utter words to her and evoke laughter. He bore the appearance of a paternal figure to her, yet their discourse was imbued with an inappropriate degree of flirtation.

I rose from my seat and engaged in social interactions, and after a brief passage of time, I shifted my gaze towards the couch, where it became apparent that Jessica was engaging in an intimate exchange with the aforementioned mature gentleman. I gazed at them with profound admiration. I have previously observed couples with disparate backgrounds, however, none had an age disparity as substantial as the one I encountered in this instance.

I returned to the couch in order to gather additional information. According to Jessica, their encounter took place during a cruise, where they developed an affectionate bond. I inquired about his personal experiences and discerned from the narratives provided that he was approximately in his eighties, making an estimation of his age. Throughout the remainder of the evening, I observed their interactions closely, and it became evident that they were sincerely content in each other's company.

Jessica was embarking upon her early stages of young adulthood, whereas he had considerably advanced into the sphere of late adulthood. I am uncertain whether she harbored ulterior motives in awaiting his demise to acquire his wealth, or if her affection for him was genuine; regardless, their relationship struck me as profoundly unconventional. A discrepancy in age of 20 years can be deemed acceptable as long as both individuals are in congruence with regards to their life stage, but a distinction of 60 years is undeniably preposterous.

Take Off Your Mask

Authentic soulmates are individuals who consistently serve as honest reflections for one another. This is because they allow each other the space and freedom to be real. Soulmates abstain from imposing expectations on one another in order to meet each other's conceptions of love. Soulmates additionally facilitate personal growth and adaptation for one another.

Maintain a steadfast dedication to prioritizing oneself, embracing true identity, embodying sincerity, and ensuring alignment between the self-projected image and genuine internal character without any incongruence. Eventually, the Law of Attraction will manifest and bring forth an authentic individual, similar to your transformed self, who will emerge as your genuine romantic partner.

REFLECTIVE EXAMINATION: Are you effectively communicating your intentions to potential partners, or are you engaging in pretense and concealing your genuine identity? Do you harbor concerns that your authentic self might not receive acceptance? Are you seeking someone who can meet the standards you have set for your idealized version of romantic affection? If the answer is affirmative, it is appropriate to remove the mask.

When you suppress or hide your true emotions, it is analogous to donning a metaphorical facade. When two individuals are incapable of expressing their authentic selves in each other's presence, yet persist in their relationship, they construct a confinement of their own devising that ultimately demands liberation. Any relationship established on falsehoods will eventually disintegrate. Joy can solely arise from affection, and affection is devoid of deception.

When one achieves clarity, one resembles a tranquil body of water wherein their reflection is mirrored flawlessly. When one's state of mind is indecisive or uncertain, they resemble a rippling body of water, wherein only fragmented aspects of their inner self are discernible.

One must display the fortitude to abandon their facade. This necessitates conveying the veracity that resonates deep within your innermost being (your elevated essence, your moral faculty) in any given circumstance, irrespective of the apprehension surrounding the potential consequences. Any foundation built upon falsehoods is inherently fragile and impermanent.

If two individuals pledge to embody authenticity, they possess the potential to cultivate a relationship that will endure the trials of time, provided they also demonstrate unwavering dedication to reciprocating the respect and treatment they themselves wish to receive. Furthermore, it is necessary to regard oneself in the same manner as one expects others to be regarded.

Being unclear entails the act of expressing or engaging in actions that deviate from the guidance of one's true emotions and inner voice, thereby forsaking and displaying a lack of confidence in one's authentic self. Each instance in which you opt for ambiguity, concealing your genuine emotions, leads to the erosion of your self-assurance, self-worth, recognition, approval, and regard.

When one abstains from placing confidence in or depending upon their own capabilities, they adorn themselves with a metaphorical mask. This erodes one's self-esteem.

One does not derive pleasure from one's own company when surrounded by individuals who deceive or feign authenticity. This undermines one's self-esteem.

You diminish your self-worth by disregarding the significance of your own opinion or personal path in life. This erodes your sense of self-worth.

You consistently exhibit a lack of self-endorsement or confidence in your own personal qualities. This undermines your sense of self-acceptance.

You do not exhibit due regard or respect for your own emotions and requirements. This undermines your sense of self-worth.

Uncertainty gives rise to feelings of culpability, repentance, accrues metaphysical obligations, as well as engenders hindrances and flaws within the individual.

The term "tear" originates from the etymological root meaning "skin" or "hide." Wearing a mask can be viewed as a means of concealing or disguising one's genuine emotions. It ultimately derives from the ancient Indo-European root sken- which connotes 'to sever, divide, or segment'.

Engaging in self-deprecating behavior is equivalent to severing a portion of one's own being. Presently, it signifies the act of dissecting or fragmenting, of cleaving through the presence of hesitation, ambiguity, and mental anguish [a conflicted psyche torn between obligations (intellect) and yearnings (emotion)].

At all times, you possess the opportunity to listen and respect your authentic inner self through clarity, or to conceal and undermine your being by adopting a facade.

The etymology of the word "tear" reveals an interesting connection to the word "sin." This association can be traced back to the Latin term "sons," which means "guilty," as well as to the Old English word "sooth," meaning "truth," and the Sanskrit term "satya," which translates to "real" or "true." Consequently, the original essence of sin can be understood as the act of being guilty for failing to speak the truth.

An alternate interpretation of the term tear pertains to the act of shedding tears, displaying expressions of sorrow, grief, and exhibiting signs of weeping. The term grief derives from the etymological origin of oppress, signifying the act of suppressing or subduing one's emotions, sentiments, or fervor. By engaging in self-deprecation, individuals generate their own emotional distress and sorrow, as they disconnect their rational thoughts from their emotional being. You become divided.

The fusion of your intellect and emotions should harmonize, akin to soulmates. Consider these aspects as complementary facets of your being, with the intellect representing the masculine and the emotions embodying the feminine.

In order to become a soulmate to someone else, it is imperative that you establish a deep connection with your own soul beforehand. True love can only be forged when two complete individuals unite. In order to attain a state of completeness, it is imperative to possess a profound understanding of one's own identity and prioritize one's own welfare above all else.

What prompts you to don a mask, to forsake your genuine identity? The answer is fear. Fear is the root cause of inhibiting one's ability to express their authentic thoughts and convictions in various circumstances, guided by the principles of their moral compass. The root cause for abstaining from love consistently lies in fear.

Emotional suffering stems from a sense of trepidation and arises when one's desires, expectations, or perceived necessities are not fulfilled. The apprehension towards pain, coupled with the longing to evade it, prompts us to conceal our emotions, disconnect from our authentic selves, and engage in deceitful and harmful behavior towards each other.

The sole outcome provided by our exercise of free will is the capacity to make choices. We cannot control everything that comes our way, but we do have the freedom to decide how we will react to it.

In essence, every decision ultimately pertains to two fundamental aspects, namely love (which represents truth) or fear (symbolizing falsehood and sin). These choices consequently give rise to two distinct outcomes, specifically action and reaction.

Fear stands as the diametric opposite of love and the fundamental source of sin. Actions driven by fear inevitably lead to pain, without exception, in due course, for the individual engaging in fearful behavior (and it is important to acknowledge that even mere thoughts hold the power of action).

This initiates a sequence of events characterized by action and reaction, as each action gives rise to a corresponding and proportionate reaction, in accordance with Newton's Third Law of Motion. This perpetual cycle will persist indefinitely, unless the doer endures such profound suffering that they no longer desire to experience it, prompting them to make an alternative decision rooted in altruistic affection rather than self-centeredness.

Opting for an altruistic affection gives rise to a cascading effect of bliss, fostering an amplification of happiness. Happiness is the outcome of selecting Love. It shall persist for as long as your choices are fueled by altruistic love.

Chapter Seven

At present, Sam and I have maintained a relationship for a duration of 7 years, with our marriage spanning 4 years. Throughout this period, we have fortunately not engaged in significant conflicts, although there have been instances when our emotions have escalated, resulting in mutual hurt.

We ensured that no derogatory language was used and that there was no animosity between us. We committed to addressing any disagreements during our evening discussion in order to resolve any lingering issues, and subsequently retired for the night.

We ensured the maintenance of a healthy relationship amidst our most challenging moments. Love held immense significance to us, which is why we devoted considerable effort to eradicating toxicity from our relationship. As our family grew and children entered the picture, we felt a sense of duty to cultivate an environment of safety for them. Even during moments of intense disagreement between Sam and myself...

Sam opted to step away for some fresh air during a conflict, deeming it more prudent than uttering irreparable hurtful remarks.

I opt to maintain composure rather than engaging in a verbal exchange with Sam.

I take great pride in the strength and depth of our relationship and marriage.

I take great pride in the depth of our mutual understanding and the significant progress we have made.

We considered it appropriate to demonstrate flexibility regarding our expectations and exerted effort to ensure mutual happiness on a daily basis.

We engage in endeavors to enhance the quality of our lives, and on occasions when I become excessively consumed by work or feel overwhelmed by the chaos of the world, he serves as the grounding influence that reorients my perspective.

Sam is my unwavering source of support during my times of emotional vulnerability.

We possess a large household that has perpetually been our aspiration.

Sam is my lifelong soulmate, as I highly question the possibility of encountering another gentleman who possesses such profound understanding and unwavering affection for me, just as I reciprocate towards him.

Similar, we harmonize exceptionally well in numerous aspects, demonstrating a remarkable synergy.

Had we experienced apprehension of abandonment or disregarded the emotions of one another, and failed to cultivate qualities of patience and compassion, I am confident that the progress we have achieved thus far would not have been possible.

The underlying message of this authentic narrative is straightforward. I encourage you to extract the key elements from my account and apply them to your own circumstances. I am confident that you will discover areas in which you can make adjustments in your romantic life, relationships, or even while being single.

It is evident;

Both Sam and I had procured

It is now an opportune moment to focus on personal growth and development.

Interactions with

mutually" "reciprocally" "in a manner that is mutually beneficial"

It is possible for you to discover the genuine, abiding love of your life and establish a deep, meaningful connection if you dedicate yourself to self-improvement.

Exercise caution before entering into another romantic commitment. Take the time to focus on personal growth and refrain from rushing into new relationships.

First and foremost, cultivate a strong sense of self-worth that will lead you towards a path filled with affection and positivity.

Finding Your True Love

Many of people face problems when they try to locate their soul mate, often leading them to give up on finding their soul mate because it didn't come about according to their terms. Individuals occasionally set a specific timeframe within their thoughts, believing that if they have not encountered their ideal life partner by that designated point in time, the possibility of meeting that person ceases to exist, conclusively. They harbor the belief that they have failed to seize their moment or opportunity. Individuals holding such perspectives have established a predetermined notion of inevitable failure, and when the stipulated deadline transpires without success, they exhibit a steadfast unwillingness to accept the potential for favorable outcomes in their favor ultimately. This approach is not conducive to the genuine discovery of your soul mate.

For the serendipitous occurrence of encountering your soulmate, it is requisite that the cosmic forces align synchronously, thereby initializing the desired enchantment. If you have already dismissed the possibility of finding a meaningful connection, closing your mind to the belief that it could still occur will undoubtedly result in the loss of your opportunity. The enchantment will occur at the opportune moment for both individuals involved, and it will transpire precisely when it is meant to occur. Its occurrence may transpire tonight or in the course of the next four years, rendering it impracticable to ascertain a preferred date and time to accommodate one's schedule. Despite having a preconceived notion of the most opportune moment to encounter your soul mate, it cannot be guaranteed that this alignment of circumstances will coincide with your convenience.

It is imperative for you to be open to the concept that, irrespective of your age, this may transpire at an entirely unforeseen moment in your life. Numerous individuals may encounter their soulmate during a period when such an occurrence was least anticipated. It is important to cultivate a mindset of patience and refrain from fixating on the timing of events. Rather, one should be open to the possibility that these desired outcomes may manifest in their future.

Acquire the capacity to derive pleasure from your existence and conduct it according to your personal preferences, finding contentment with your self-identity. By doing so, you may facilitate a more expeditious and effortless realization of desirable outcomes. When one encounters their soul mate, it will unfailingly transpire due to their embodiment of the qualities that their prospective partner earnestly seeks in a devoted and affectionate life companion. One way to enhance your chances of finding a life partner is by yielding to the subtle prompts that your mind occasionally presents. If you perceive an intuition indicating that your usual commute to work may not be advisable, I would advise trusting your instincts and opting for an alternative route. If unexpectedly there arises an inclination within your mind to venture on a leisurely stroll through the park today, I implore you to heed this internal prompting and proceed with a perambulation amidst the park's serene environs. This fortuitous decision may yield unforeseen encounters, perchance even leading to the auspicious discovery of your compatible companion. I dare assert that you shall be astonished by the profound potentiality harbored within your cerebral faculties, for they possess a remarkable resonance with the external milieu, surpassing their perceived limitations.

The intricate network of electrical waves permeates our collective existence, interconnecting each individual. When one achieves a heightened state of attunement with their brain waves, the mind has the capacity to place individuals in extraordinary circumstances that may appear seemingly fantastical.

Striking Up Good Conversations. To encounter your ideal life partner, you will need to initiate a meaningful exchange with them at some juncture. Engaging in dialogue may either be effortless or challenging, contingent upon the individuals partaking. If the individual you are attempting to establish a connection with exhibits disinterest and demonstrates no inclination to foster a connection with you, it is prudent to consider that this may not be the suitable individual for you, notwithstanding any superficial attraction that may exist presently. When considering the concept of a soul mate, one will find that they possess an impactful inner beauty that fosters a profound connection, extending beyond mere physical attraction. When searching for a compatible life partner, it is crucial to uncover individuals' preferences and aversions in order to determine whether there is potential for shared values and interests conducive to developing a lasting relationship.

Once a positive rapport has been established, you may experience a sense of readiness to disclose and establish a deeper connection with this individual, fostering a desire to cultivate a more robust bond. Through conversing, individuals gradually develop a sense of ease and familiarity with one another. They are capable of initiating the establishment of trust through conversational interactions. Engaging in meaningful discourse can ultimately lead you to encounter your ideal life partner. Allow me to present you with some suggestions for facilitating constructive dialogues with individuals:

Extend an invitation for individuals to narrate their experiences - be sure to inquire with open-ended queries that prompt comprehensive responses rather than mere affirmation or denial. Allow them to respond to your inquiries and ensure that you are attentive and fully engaged with their responses. Strive to present yourself as fully engaged and attentive, conveying genuine interest in the individual's discourse, while avoiding any appearance of distraction or preoccupation. Engaging in activities such as checking your phone or surveying the surroundings whilst someone is sharing a narrative is remarkably impolite. Females, in particular, are likely to be deterred by such behavior or attitude.

Share your narrative with the individual — discourse is a reciprocal encounter. If an individual discloses their identity, it is appropriate to reciprocate by revealing your own identity. It is unnecessary to divulge your complete life history all at once to them. Reserve a few of your anecdotes for a subsequent occasion. If both parties share a genuine mutual interest, this progression will occur organically. Kindly acquaint the individual with fundamental aspects pertaining to your person, such as your personal interests, professional occupation, hobbies, and similar preferences. Once you have established a certain level of personal disclosure with this individual, the subsequent exchange of ideas and discussion should transition effortlessly from one topic to the next. Permit the individual to become acquainted with you to the extent that you desire to become acquainted with them.

Engage in preparations — to mitigate any potential discomfort, make an effort to conduct research on the individual you find intriguing. One must exercise caution and strive to avoid behaving peculiarly in order to prevent inadvertently appearing like a stalker to the individual in question. Engage in this task ahead of time to proactively circumvent potential obstacles. Conduct a thorough inquiry of their social media profiles, namely on platforms such as Twitter, Facebook, and others of the like. Merely by perusing these accounts, one can glean insight into their character and discern their areas of interest.

Establish meaningful and genuine connections with individuals to the fullest extent possible, without compromising your authenticity. This involves exerting a modest amount of effort to steer the conversation towards a positive trajectory. It is imperative that you engage in discussions with the individual in a manner that avoids contentious arguments, as failure to do so may result in severing ties with them. Investigate the rationale behind their beliefs and the underlying factors influencing their perspectives. This is an effective method of acquainting oneself with an individual. Typically, the majority of couples do not share identical beliefs, as they maintain distinct perspectives on various aspects of life by virtue of their individuality. Discrepancies in certain areas of opinion should not preclude the possibility of forming a mutually satisfying and harmonious partnership.

Please be attentive – although you may have encountered this advice countless times, it is genuinely crucial to attentively listen to the individual speaking, as it may not always be a facile task. It is essential to attentively engage and actively listen when someone is speaking in order to gain a deeper understanding of their perspectives and experiences. You have the opportunity to acquire information that may prove useful in the future. In the event that the individual informs you of their milk allergy and subsequently, approximately ten minutes later, you extend an offer to provide them with a milkshake, it conveys a lack of attentiveness or attentiveness to their earlier disclosure. You may potentially incur a significant deduction of points for such behavior, as it is crucial for an individual to perceive genuine attentiveness towards the information they are sharing. By attentively listening to someone, you can discern whether their conversation aligns with your values and qualities, helping you determine if they have the potential to be your life partner.

Active listening is crucial and can be demonstrated by affirmatively nodding in response to the speaker's discourse. This will serve to reassure the individual that you are fully attentive to their needs. You may exhibit suitable facial expressions as a means to demonstrate your comprehension and engagement with the subject matter being discussed.

Familiarize yourself with the appropriate inquiries — for initial engagements, gather insights on their interests and pastimes by posing relevant questions. It is advisable to refrain from inquiring about overly personal or sensitive matters during the initial interaction with an individual. Engaging in such behavior is likely to deter numerous individuals, thereby significantly impeding the process of establishing a meaningful connection during the initial stages of acquaintance. When seeking a life partner, it is imperative to establish a deep connection with their inner being, in order to discern the compatibility between your souls.

Delve further - once you have engaged in multiple prior conversations with an individual, it is permissible to now explore the conversation on a deeper level. One can initiate the process of uncovering their strengths, fears, and weaknesses. At this juncture, you are gradually acquainting yourself with the individual on a more profound level. You are not merely acquiring knowledge about the individual, but rather, you are truly acquainting yourself with their authentic self and delving into the core aspects that drive their personality. Furthermore, it is opportune to disclose an aspect of your personal life within the context of this situation. It is essential to bear in mind that, for a conversation to yield fruitful results, both parties must engage in a collaborative and concerted effort to actively participate and contribute.

It is advisable not to explicitly express your impressive qualities and accomplishments, as individuals who genuinely recognize your greatness and excellence are likely to have already acknowledged them. It is considered lacking in refinement to excessively boast of one's abilities or flaunt them in an ostentatious manner. The majority of individuals harbor a strong disapproval towards this. It is highly probable that you will be perceived as impolite and conceited, which are generally unappealing traits for individuals seeking a life partner. Please provide an introduction about yourself without explicitly emphasizing your exceptional qualities.

Make an effort to maintain a coherent flow of ideas, as abrupt transitions between thoughts may evoke a sense of being interrogated in the individual.

When an individual responds to a query, refrain from immediately transitioning to a completely disconnected subject by posing another question. Engage in further inquiry by posing additional questions on the same subject matter, or provide your response subsequent to their contribution. Engaging in a meaningful dialogue would be rather difficult if your manner of communication solely consists of incessant questioning. Each and every one of you should have an opportunity to speak.

Sealing The Deal

If you receive a response from any of the women to whom you have sent messages, it is important to maintain composure in order to preserve the momentum you have established. Merely receiving indications of a girl's interest does not automatically signify accomplishment on your part; it is imperative to solidify the connection. However, what precise methodology can be employed to further embed the hook?

Remain composed and extend gratitude

As previously stated, it is essential to maintain composure in order to avoid an excessive reaction when composing your response. Your message should effectively convey your appreciation for her response, demonstrating gratitude for the time she took to reply. However, it is important to strike a balance and refrain from excessive expressions of gratitude, as this may potentially discourage or disinterest her. A mere expression of gratitude will be adequate.

Initiating a Dialogue and Strategies for Sustaining Engagement

Afterwards, it is advisable to disclose certain aspects of your life to her, while being cautious not to delve too deeply into the specifics at this stage. Save those details for when you have the opportunity to meet face-to-face. At this moment, a brief summary of your current occupation and personal interests would suffice. In addition, it is imperative to inquire about the preferences of the other party. Once more, it is advisable to abstain from posing overly specific queries. The purpose of these inquiries is to acquire supplementary information to initiate and sustain a meaningful conversation.

If you discover that you share certain similarities, such as common pet peeves or shared hobbies and interests, you can employ this knowledge in your subsequent message to pique her further interest.

Requesting a Face-to-Face Meeting

It is customary for you to personally meet the woman who has piqued your interest on the online dating platform, yet it is advisable to approach this encounter artfully to avoid any major complications.

To begin with, it would not be advisable to arrange a meeting with the young lady shortly after her initial response. Pursuing this course of action would be highly inadvisable as you are proceeding at an excessive pace. Given the limited extent of her acquaintance with you, she does not possess an adequate level of trust necessary to agree to a meeting. It is advisable to primarily communicate through emails or chat rooms at this stage (obtaining her personal phone number appears improbable at this early phase). Utilize this opportunity to gradually establish trust with her, and eventually, she might even initiate a suggestion to meet for coffee or lunch.

It would be beneficial for you to utilize this opportunity to further acquaint yourself with the woman whom you have a vested interest in. The information disclosed on an individual's online profile offers limited insight into their character; a more comprehensive understanding can be attained through engaging in a profound conversation with them.

The crucial aspect lies in demonstrating patience; it is imperative to adapt oneself to the girl's tempo instead of imposing one's will upon her. Exhibiting undue haste can yield unfavorable outcomes if not exercised with caution; it may either cause the girl to lose interest in your demeanor or result in a partnership where complete compatibility is lacking.

Do you smoke? Do you drink?

I have refrained from smoking and I have an aversion to the scent emanating from individuals who engage in smoking or currently cigarette consumption. When searching for a partner, it was imperative to find a man who abstains from smoking, does not engage in excessive alcohol consumption, and refrains from any detrimental habits that I cannot tolerate. The potential involvement of a smoker in a prospective romantic relationship has the potential to pose some challenges, especially if you are a non-smoker. However, if the individual's smoking habits do not inherently trouble or distress you, such concerns may be mitigated.

On certain occasions, when perusing an online profile, the information pertaining to an individual's smoking habits may be absent, and only during email exchanges or online conversations with one's virtual acquaintance does this particular detail come to light. If one does not engage in smoking and is seeking a non-smoking partner, it would be advisable to communicate this preference beforehand. In my experience, I have encountered couples wherein only one member engages in smoking. It is notable that, over the course of the relationship, it is not uncommon for the non-smoking partner to make efforts in persuading the smoker to quit, consequently leading to substantial disagreements in the future.

A substantial number of individuals frequent pubs on weekends, seeking opportunities to socialize with friends and indulge in alcoholic beverages. However, a clear distinction exists between consuming alcohol in moderation and engaging in excessive drinking. When I pursued online dating, it came to light that my potential partner and I shared an affinity for alcohol, but limited our consumption to social gatherings or noteworthy occasions.

It is disconcerting when an individual candidly discloses their weekend engagements, which consistently involve excessive levels of alcohol consumption and subsequent return home inebriated. Furthermore, the nonchalant manner in which this information is conveyed suggests that your online acquaintance has a predilection for drinking. Therefore, it would be prudent to inquire about the manner in which your cyber friend spends their weekends and whether they frequently partake in social outings with companions. If your intention is to form a long-term companionship, it is advisable to consider acquainting yourself with individuals who maintain good health and abstain from detrimental behaviors. It is essential to exercise caution when engaging with individuals who have a history of drug abuse or those who have undergone rehabilitation. It is plausible that you may come across an acquaintance in the online realm who openly expresses an affinity for visiting gambling establishments, or they may have previously struggled with alcohol dependency. Nevertheless, they assert a transformation in their conduct and share their pursuit of a fresh existence. Engaging with individuals who possess or have exhibited detrimental behaviors carries inherent risks, as the prospects of a future relationship remain uncertain and there exists the potential for its consequential dissolution.

Health

There could be numerous motivations behind an individual concealing their health condition when seeking a partner through online platforms. Given the nature of their situation, it proves challenging for them to discuss it openly. It is possible that your online acquaintance refrains from disclosing their affliction, as it pertains to a chronic or hereditary illness. This might be due to his reluctance to potentially endanger the strong bond of friendship that already exists between you both; however, entertaining such thoughts would be incorrect. Indeed, it is advisable to engage in discussions pertaining not only to the well-being of your acquaintances in the cyber realm, but also to your own physical condition. Particularly if there has been a prolonged correspondence and a mutual interest has developed, with genuine contemplation of a future face-to-face encounter.

In the event that any individual experiences a medical condition, wherein there exists mutual comprehension, it behooves you to openly communicate about the nature of said medical condition, for it will foster a supportive environment amongst yourselves. For example, there could be a situation where your cyberfriend or maybe you have diabetes, or suffers from epilepsy, in both cases people with those conditions must follow a treatment and have a normal life like anybody else, they could live happily with their partners because since the very beginning they shared with their partner about their medical condition. However, there may arise additional challenges and unique circumstances. For instance, an individual may experience infertility resulting in their inability to conceive, thereby harboring apprehension in disclosing this matter to their significant other. In actuality, instances have occurred where individuals have become betrothed, subsequently wedded, and encountered challenges with reproductive capabilities, all while keeping this matter undisclosed to their significant other.

My mother played a crucial role in providing extensive support during my quest for a potential partner through the Internet. She told me how important it is to know if my cyberfriend was healthy and I am the one who one day asked Mark if he suffered a medical condition, I asked him many questions regarding illnesses and if he had them when he was a child, asked if he had allergies, or if he had ever suffered of a serious illness, that way I knew that he and his family did not have a history of medical problems.

We seek an individual who possesses good health, which encompasses both physical well-being and mental wellness. Therefore, we kindly request you to ascertain that your cyberfriend does not experience symptoms of depression. Individuals may experience significant adverse effects from depression and therefore require specialized medication, as it possesses the potential to detrimentally impact and prove to be detrimental to their romantic relationship.

The Divorced Ones

Individuals who have undergone a separation or divorce have endured a profoundly challenging period in their lives, and they will inevitably reach a juncture where they opt to progress and embark on new relationships, including engaging in dating activities. The online dating platforms host a significant number of individuals who have undergone a divorce and are prepared to embark upon a fresh chapter in their lives with a new companion. In the event that both you and your digital acquaintance have encountered divorce, it is advisable to engage in a discussion regarding your respective matrimonial experiences and the factors that contributed to the dissolution of your marriages.

A close acquaintance of mine recently underwent a challenging and intricate separation process, yet she exhibited resilience and actively sought solace in the unwavering presence of her son. Subsequently, she embarked upon a search for a companion through an Online Dating Platform, ultimately encountering the gentleman who presently serves as her spouse, concurrently encompassing children from a prior union. They have both moved on from their past and their children have formed a positive rapport with each other, resulting in their current cohabitation as a blended family.

Certain individuals have undergone divorce and maintain amicable relations with their former spouses. This is attributable to their shared understanding and commitment to prioritize the well-being of their children. However, the extent to which such agreeable terms can be established is contingent upon the circumstances leading to the dissolution of their relationship. Additionally, there are individuals who have undergone a challenging divorce characterized by a protracted process of reaching a mutual understanding and engaging in a legal dispute over the custody of their children. Financial assets and personal possessions may also become contested in the process of divorce.

There exist numerous factors which contribute to the challenges faced by individuals who have undergone divorce in initiating new relationships, such as diminished self-assurance resulting from a previous marital failure or instances of manipulation by one's former spouse and children.

One may encounter the possibility of establishing a virtual friendship with an individual who exhibits genuine interest in their unique personality, while also disclosing that they have undergone a divorce and are presently raising a child. Should this be true and if he has bestowed his trust upon you from the onset regarding his current situation and divulged the details of his past romantic involvement, it may signify his genuine interest in you and his willingness to further acquaint himself with you. The decision as to whether you wish to establish a solely platonic relationship with your cyberfriend or entertain the possibility of him being a potential romantic partner rests solely in your hands. Should the latter be the case, it would be prudent to acquaint yourself with him on a deeper level and ascertain the reasons behind the failure of his previous relationship.

Prospects of Parenthood or a Childless Existence

During the course of acquainting oneself with each other, various topics will inevitably be broached, among which the subject of children shall feature prominently. Perhaps this possibility may arise if your virtual acquaintance has transitioned into becoming your virtual romantic partner, and you engage in discussions pertaining to future prospects. Do you both possess a mutual inclination towards desiring to establish a family in the forthcoming days, and do you both harbor affinity towards children? Alternatively, could it be the case that you have no inclination towards engaging with children whatsoever?

Individuals who have children stemming from a prior union may express a desire to form a new partnership, thereby pursuing matrimony and potentially expanding their family. However, it is important to acknowledge that there are those who hold divergent perspectives, opting against further parenthood.

It will become apparent whether your online partner harbors an affinity for children if he begins conversing with you about his nieces or nephews, relishing their company, taking them to the cinema, and even sharing pictures of them with you."

Allow me to present the scenario of Daniela, who cohabited with her partner for a duration exceeding a decade, exhibiting unwavering dedication to one another throughout, yet never formalizing their union through matrimony. As time elapsed, the topic of parenthood remained untouched between them; they never engaged in a dialogue concerning this matter. One day, Daniela's significant other engaged in infidelity, leading her to comprehend that their cohabitation was driven by routine rather than genuine affection. Upon this discovery, Daniela came to the realization that she harbored a genuine desire to become a parent. Sadly, the opportune moment had already passed, prompting her to reluctantly accept the notion of forgoing motherhood due to her partner's lack of interest. Following the dissolution of their relationship, Daniela made the choice to seek a suitable companion on an Online Dating

Site, with the specific intention of finding an individual who shared her aspirations of establishing a family.

During our correspondence via email, Mark and I discussed the prospect of establishing a family at some point in the future. We were immensely delighted to discover our shared aspiration of parenthood in the future, and recognized the significance of meticulous timing in the process of planning for it.

The choice of having children necessitates mutual agreement between two individuals, given its significant responsibility and the requirement for deep love and understanding within the couple.

www.ingramcontent.com/pod-product-compliance
Lightning Source LLC
Chambersburg PA
CBHW050248120526
44590CB00016B/2257